Growing Cannabis Indoors

Grow Your Own Marijuana Indoors Using This Easy-to-Follow Guide
(2022 Crash Course for Beginners)

Terry Twitty

Table of Contents

The Basics of Cannabis

The majority of individuals use marijuana for two reasons: medicinal and recreational.

Tetrahydrocannabinol (THC) is the psychoactive component of marijuana that causes users to experience a high. THC levels vary from plant to plant, and a good powerful plant contains both high amounts and levels of THC.

THC levels are genetically set and cannot be influenced. However, THC quantities are variable and include your weed's bud mass and the amount of resin it can produce. Always examine the THC levels when purchasing cannabis seeds, since this will decide the potential strength of your marijuana plants.

Cannabidiol is another key characteristic (CBD). This characteristic is responsible for the amplifying and depressing effects of THC. THC and CBD contain molecular formulas that are similar but not structurally identical. CBD does not have psychoactive qualities and cannot accomplish anything on its own, but it does moderate THC's euphoric effects, giving it a calming impact.

Marijuana seeds are often a crossbreed of the two primary marijuana strains, indica, and Sativa. Strains are what distinguish various marijuana specimens by imparting distinct and distinct traits.

Grow a Sativa dominant cannabis for a more active high due to its high THC and low CBD levels. Because of its high CBD levels, Indica dominated cannabis is excellent for a more relaxed high.

Let's take a closer look at the two primary strains:

Cannabis Indica

Morocco, Tibet, and Afghanistan are the origins of Cannabis Indica.

Indica plants are short and thick, with wide, round, and pointed leaves with no patterning. They mostly develop into dark green plants. They take 6 to 8 weeks to completely develop after blooming and produce thick and dense buds with a powerful odor.

Indica plants are strong and, when compared to Sativa, can withstand colder temperature conditions. They are simple to cultivate and mature into short, thick, vigorous, and bushy plants that need enough space.

Indica strains are the finest for indoor production because of these qualities. If you want to grow Indica cannabis indoors, the finest producing strains are

Blue Berries, White Rhino, Sensi Star, and Critical.

Plants from this strain have lower THC and greater CBD levels as compared to Sativas (we shall learn more about this later), and as a result of these traits, when smoked, they produce a heavy, stony, and boring drowsy effect. Their cigarette smoke is very dense. Indica strains are useful for medicinal applications since they have lower THC

and greater CBD levels.

12

Cannabis Sativa

Sativa strains develop to be tall plants (100-200 cm). The strain is said to have originated in Mexico, Thailand, Colombia, and Southeast Asia. Cannabis sativa has slender, rounded, finger-like leaves with marble-like patterns and short internodes between branches (about 3 inches).

13

Cannabis sativa plants develop quite quickly. They may take 14 to 16 weeks to develop after blooming, yielding buds with a sweet and fruity aroma. They also create smoke that is smooth and simple to inhale. Sativa plants have greater THC levels and quantity but lower CBD levels than Cannabis Indica plants, giving consumers an active, clear, and buzzy high.

Sativa plants have less chlorophyll but more accessory pigments (the material that defends the plant from too much sunshine), and as a result, they need more light.

Sativa is tough to produce indoors because of its height needs and blooming habits. If you want some of its qualities in your indoor marijuana, though, you may cross it with Indica.

15

A Sativa/Indica hybrid will produce huge plants that are shorter than Sativa plants. Their THC levels are lower and their CBD levels are somewhat greater than Sativa's. If you want to produce Sativa in your grow room, use the Northern-Light strain since it is simpler to grow indoors.

If you want to learn how to grow marijuana indoors, start with the Indica species since it is simple to cultivate and will therefore make the process of producing marijuana easier as you learn more about it. As you acquire skill, you may experiment with Indica/Sativa hybrids before moving on to a pure Sativa strain.

To acquire the highest yield, you need to be aware of the following:

Sexing

The technique of detecting whether a marijuana plant is female or male is known as weed sexing. This method is only feasible at the blossoming stage since it is only then that the difference may be seen.

Female marijuana plants generate teardrop-shaped balls or buds called calyxes at the nodes located between stems and leaves, but male marijuana plants make small buds or balls without white hairs at the terminals of the branches where buds are expected to grow. With each emerging white hair, these balls will grow closer together.

19

Because male plants contain low quantities of cannabinoids, most marijuana farmers remove them from their plants (THC and CBD). To prevent pollination, sex your plants as soon as the blooms appear.

Pollinated flowers will devote the majority of their energy to seed production, resulting in poor quality, filthy cannabis (seedy weed is a dirty weed) with low levels of cannabinoids.

If your female marijuana plants do not get pollination, they will devote the majority of their energy to the budding stage, generating buds with a high resin content and consequently a greater potency. Buds and flowers are the only parts of the marijuana plant that may be

21

used for medical or recreational reasons.

Breeders have generated feminized cannabis cultivars due to the qualities present in female marijuana plants. This implies they will mature and develop feminine traits.

Creating an Indoor Grow Room

Now that you're familiar with the typical marijuana jargon with which you'll come into contact when cultivating marijuana, the following step is to set up your grow room. Planning the following key things/subjects will be required while setting up your indoor marijuana grow room:

Security is the first step.

Indoor marijuana growing is extremely safe from herbivores, insects, illnesses, and many other elements that might impact your plants since you have total control over the growing environment; if you optimize this advantage, your pot plants will offer you the greatest results possible.

Indoor grow rooms also safeguard you from unfair laws. Even in locations where growing medicinal marijuana is allowed, it is critical to keep your grow room hidden for a variety of reasons, including thieves.

26

If you are in trouble and the cops arrive at your home, do not allow them in unless they have a search warrant. The legislation forbids officers from entering a residence or even a car without a search warrant or sufficient cause.

You must be aware of the following security standards as a cannabis grower:

The first rule is "never tell anybody you cultivate marijuana."

According to estimates, roughly 1% of indoor marijuana farmers are in difficulty with the law just because they divulged to others that they had a grow room. Trust no one and keep your grow chamber hidden.

The second rule is "never sell marijuana." Never take money for marijuana and only give it out for free since doing so will draw attention and lead to legal troubles. You may share your marijuana with your buddies, but you should never tell them you cultivated it. They may be trustworthy, but humans are people, and as such, they are prone to mistakes that might lead to unanticipated consequences.

Always have a ready-made tale to tell them since they will most likely ask where you got it or if they can purchase it.

Step 2: Make More Room Space

The minimum marijuana grows room size should be 20 square feet "long x 24" wide x 48" tall Weed plants will not need all of this area at first; but, as they grow/develop, this space will become advantageous (especially the height).

You may use a non-working refrigerator, an old cabinet, or even a spare closet if you don't have an empty room to grow your cannabis in. The following are the essential criteria that

31

must be modified to produce a decent grow room:

Electricity

Electricity should be available in your grow room since you will need it to power equipment such as a fan, a light source, and other tiny gadgets. One outlet is sufficient, and it may be connected to a grounded power strip with at least six plugs and surge protection.

In your grow chamber, you will have access to both water and electricity, and everyone knows that the two should never be mixed. Keep all electrical plugs off the floor to decrease the possibility of contact with water if it spills when watering to prevent starting an electrical fire.

New Breath of Life

All living things need fresh air, and since marijuana plants are living creatures, they require a constant supply of fresh air. If you believe your room isn't getting enough fresh air due to limited ventilation holes or windows, invest in a vent fan.

Intake and return vents are required for a refrigerator or armoire. Place the intake vent towards the bottom of your non-working fridge or armoire, and the return vent near the top, where the light warm air will collect.

A vent fan in your grow room will not only offer fresh air to your plants but will also aid in temperature and humidity management.

Light Resistant

35

Your plant will ultimately begin to blossom. They will be photosensitive at this time. Your plants should be kept in a dark room or environment at this time. If you can still see your hands after shutting the door and pulling the window curtains, your grow room needs attention. Your growing space must be dark.

To hide the margins of the door or windows, use thick plastics such as panda film or Mylar tape to seal off the light. The greatest film is Panda because it has one black side and one white side. The white side will be on the inside to assist reflect light onto the plants for development, while the black side will be facing the entrance or window to prevent outside light from entering the space.

Flat white paint, reflective Mylar, or Panda film are the ideal reflecting materials to utilize in your room. Mirrors are not light reflectors; rather, they are absorbers that will absorb a large portion of the light required by your plants. As a result, avoid using any mirrors.

Step 3: Choosing a Growing Medium

Hydroponics is the most effective and efficient method of growing marijuana indoors. This entails planting your marijuana in the absence of soil. According to studies, producing pot hydroponically is.25 percent quicker than growing it on soil and generates high-quality marijuana.

Hydroponics keeps your grow space clean, makes maintenance easy, and allows you to leave your plants alone for several days if you are busy or traveling. Many different kinds of hydro systems may be used for indoor marijuana cultivation. They are as follows:

Deep Water Culture (DWC)

It is the most basic hydro system, and most growers describe it as a bubbler.

To build the Deep Water Culture hydro system, fill a large plastic container with water, such as a 5-gallon bucket with a cover or a 12-gallon Tupperware container. The benefit of huge pots is that they may house a large number of plants that will all get the same quantity of nutrients.

The DWC reservoir must be opaque so that light does not enter the water and encourages the development of algae that competes for nutrients. Connect an airline from a small aquarium air pump feed to the reservoir to keep the water oxygenated so your plants don't die. Submerge the hosepipe in water by putting a rock or any other inert weight on it. To secure the rock to the pipe, use a thread or a plastic zip tie.

Make 3.75-inch circular holes in the container lid "net pots made of plastic Fill these plastic net pots with little hydroton grow pebbles, which will help keep the plant in place. These may be reused forever.

To plant the marijuana, put 1 to 3 started plants in 1.5 liters of the soil "Rockwool cubes should be nestled within the grow rocks. Rockwool cubes are inert materials that, because of their high moisture retention, provide an excellent growth medium for marijuana seedlings.

At least once a week, add liquid fertilizers and water to the reservoir.

44

Measure the pH of the water (it should be between 5 and 6) and, if it is not in that range, fix it since failing to do so might create deficiencies in your plants.

NOTE: You may reduce the pH level by adding citric acids, such as lemon or orange juice, and increase it by using baking soda. Always keep in mind that everything added to the water alters the pH level, and to prevent difficulties caused by over-correction, you must be cautious while correcting it.

Nutrients are the fourth step.

There are many various kinds of liquid hydroponic nutrients; for example, the nutrients for the vegetative and blooming phases change because they employ different amounts of nutrients from previous stages. You do not,

46

however, need to overcomplicate the developing process. Throughout the growth phase, you may utilize a one-part, full-spectrum nutrient, such as synthetic nutrients. This will provide excellent results.

Too many nutrients in the reservoir (particularly for young plants) may burn your plants, causing the roots to wither and the leaves to become brown and crispy.

You may believe that if you feed your plants a lot of nutrients, they would produce a lot of fruit; however, this is not the case. Plants can only absorb a certain number of nutrients at a given pace. If the nutrition box recommends adding 2 or 3 teaspoons per gallon, this is the highest rate for fully developed marijuana plants. New seedlings will need no more than one-tenth of the specified rate, and as they develop, gradually increase the nutrient rate and give them time to adapt from one feeding to the next.

If your marijuana plants seem robust, healthy, and have dark green leaves, you do not need to be concerned about nutritional deficiencies.

Lighting is the fifth step.

A lighting system is required for your indoor marijuana grow area. This might be the most costly and important piece of equipment. There are several varieties of grow lights on the market today.

LED grow lights are the greatest lighting system since they employ advanced technology. LED grow lights utilize less power and generate less heat than traditional kinds of grow lights. They are also smaller and have a longer life cycle when compared to conventional grow lights.

A 90-watt LED grow lamp will provide adequate light for a 10 square foot grow area. Fix a robust bolt into the ceiling and hang a tiny chain that allows you to easily adjust the LED to the right height to install the grow light system in your grow room.

An electric timer will be required to control the amount of time the grow light will be on. Because of the bright blue and red hues of the LEDs, you may have difficulties seeing colors properly, particularly while working on the plants.

A standard source of light is required to improve vision; a reading lamp will suffice. Always switch it off once you finish working in the grow room since, although moderate, such light may generate excess heat or even interrupt the lighting cycle during the blooming period.

6th Step: Odor Control

You must regulate the marijuana stench emanating from your grow room since cannabis plants emit a strong, unique odor. The intensity of the stench will vary depending on the stage. Regardless, you will need to manage it if you do not want your house to smell 'weedy' or to have to answer a lot of queries regarding the scent.

Marijuana stench may be mitigated to some extent by using fragrant incense, candles, and air fresheners to conceal it. Even so, some individuals will be able to detect the odor, which means you'll need to develop better strategies to hide the odor. There are two effective methods for odor management. They include:

Filters made of charcoal

These are air filters that are fitted to the return vent and use charcoal to catch marijuana odor particles. Charcoal filters will need to be replaced from time to time, but the good news is that they are safe to use in an air-ventilated grow room.

Generator of Ozone

An ozone generator is a kind of electrical equipment that produces ozone.

Ozone is made up of three oxygen molecules that are linked together and are formed in the atmosphere by lights. It binds to the molecules of marijuana odor, effectively neutralizing them. Although this procedure is quite successful, it is very dangerous to your respiratory system if utilized for an

extended period.

58

Growing a Plant from Seed to Weed

You have now completed the setup of your grow room, and it is ready for planting.

Most growers make one error during the growing process that you should avoid at all costs: do not germinate your seeds in one medium and then transfer them to another medium for developing since this approach often harms your plants. Weed plant damage during the germination and growth phases may be fatal or harmful.

Implement the following procedure to germinate your seeds and care for them throughout the developing period until you harvest your weed.

Stage of Seed Germination

Place one Rockwool cube at a depth of no more than 1 cm in your reservoir/s that have plastic net pots filled with grow rocks on the lid, then take 2 or 2 marijuana seeds and put them in each Rockwool cube.

The rationale for two or three seeds in one Rockwool is to guarantee that you have numerous plants following sexing. Plant the seeds with the pointy end pointing downwards if feasible, since this is where your marijuana roots will develop.

Press the Rockwool around the seeds to ensure they are in touch with the growth media and so get all of the germination elements. If you're cultivating a variety of strains, name the Rockwool or even put a stick with a sticker behind or in front of the Rockwool so you know which strain is growing there.

To guarantee that your seeds are completely saturated, fill the reservoir with clean water up to 14 of the Rockwool cubes. Maintain a warm temperature (at least 240 degrees Celsius) by keeping the grow light on and making sure the air pump is in place and operating correctly.

You must begin your developing notebook right now. If you believe that keeping a grow log is unnecessary, you are mistaken. It is critical to make a record of what happened at each encounter since doing so will prevent you from having difficulty monitoring the number of nutrients provided, when, and other crucial data you are prone to forgetting.

After you've planted your seeds, give them a week or two to make sure they get enough water, are at the proper temperature and get at least 18 hours of sunshine every day. You might be tempted to test the seed by poking around in the Rockwool cubes.

Resist such a temptation because it will harm the developing, fragile roots. Wait for 7 to 10 days before thoroughly inspecting the seeds.

Stage of the Seedling

We refer to seedlings when they emerge from the ground after the seeds have germinated. Split-open seeds may or may not cover the plant's top. Either technique is OK since they will fall away as the leaves develop. During this stage, you are likely to encounter various issues that are inherent in the weed-growing process.

The first issue may arise when the seedlings get confused, causing the pointed white tip of the roots to emerge instead of the leaves. In this situation, gently spread open the Rockwool, flip the seedling to allow the right side to show, and then delicately press the Rockwool around the seedling, leaving just the tip end of the seed visible. Your seedlings are quite sensitive at this time; thus, be as careful as possible.

Another issue arises when the inner membrane of the seed hull fails to separate, retaining the leaves inside. If you have waited a few days and nothing has occurred, the seedlings may want your very careful assistance.

Stage of Development

69

This stage begins when the seedlings establish roots and the first pair of leaves appear and ends when the plants are ready to generate buds.

During this stage, reduce your grow light and set it about 8 inches away from the plants "above the seedlings' crowns Adjust the light location to maintain the spacing as the plants develop. You may now begin using an electronic timer to guarantee that the light operates on a 24-hour cycle.

You may want to keep the light on for 24 hours, but marijuana seedlings, like all living things, need that one-hour break. Furthermore, giving your plants this hour of rest can help them acclimatize more easily throughout the blooming period.

71

After the second or third pair of leaves appear, apply one-tenth of the required quantity of fertilizers. The rate may then be progressively increased by adding another 1/10th of the suggested amount every 4 or 5 days.

When your plants are about 8 inches tall, you may begin using a method known as Low-Stress Training (LST). LST is the method of gently bending immature marijuana plants and securing them in the bent position using strings and wires. This reduces the height of your plants while allowing light to reach more parts of the plants.

Keep in mind that the best plants are quite delicate, and some branches or stems may easily shatter. If the stems crack apart, rub some honey over the cut to help it heal quicker.

At this point, you may add a carbon dioxide source to your grow room since your plants are developing quickly and the carbon dioxide in the room may not be sufficient for their fast growth.

Plants breathe CO2 and adding it to the grow chamber may boost growth and production. If you do not add CO2, you may find that certain plants die as a result of a shortage of CO2.

At this time, your plants are fast-growing and absorbing a lot of water. Some marijuana producers empty the reservoir to change the water at various points throughout the growing cycle. That is a lot of pointless labor. Instead of changing the water, just add extra water to the reservoir when it reaches about a quarter of its capacity, and then add the proper quantity of fertilizers.

Cloning

Only during the vegetative stage, when the plants are approximately 12 inches tall, may you remove a branch and start a new plant without using seed. The marijuana plant branches you remove are known as clones because they are genetic clones of the parent plants.

76

Cut with a sharp razor to avoid causing undue stress to the plant.

If you want to have a mother plant from which to clone, the vegetative stage is the best time to do it. Allowing a designated mother clone to enter the flowering stage is never a good idea because clones cut during the flowering stage do not thrive. When clones from the Sativa strain are compared to clones from the Indica strain, they perform well.

How to Make a Clone

Cloning:

1. Choose a single woody branch on the bottom side of a plant with several leaf nodes.

2. Sterilize your hand, a razor, and a chopping block with rubbing alcohol.

3. With the razor held at a 45-degree angle, cut and then remove the branch from the mother plant. Dip the cut end in cold water right away to avoid the capillary action of the branch from drawing air, which might create issues.

4. You may separate the branch into multiple small stems by performing a series of 45-degree cuts across the nodes. Each stem is unique, should have a top and bottom (cut at 45 degrees) as well as a leaf

5. Holding a clone by the leaf stem, scrape away the outer layer of the stem to reveal the phloem on the end that will be planted as the root.

6. Apply rooting hormone or cloning gel to the scraped stem and place it in a damp Rockwool to keep the leaf upright.

7. Keep the clone humid by covering it with a glass dome or transparent plastic paper, and keep the clone and the inside of the dome wet at all times.

8. Use a windowsill with indirect light or a fluorescent desk lamp to illuminate

your clones' grow area. Direct sunlight and grow lights should be avoided since they are too powerful for young clones.

9. After around 7 days, your clone will produce roots, and if you remove the dome for several hours and the clones do not wilt, this is a good indication that they have enough roots to maintain themselves.

Stage of Flowering

When your marijuana plants reach 12 inches in height, they grow very quickly, and if left unchecked, their growth can spiral out of control.

Allow the marijuana plants to grow to a height of half the vertical space between the reservoir and the bottom of the grow lamp (when it is set to the maximum suspendable level) since when they reach the blooming stage, they will fast double in size and you may end up with unmanageable weeds.

Starting the 12/12 flowering light cycle at a young age is what many growers refer to as Sea of Green (SOG), so named because almost all weed plants in the grow room are the same height. The goal of this method is to harvest several small plants in a short period.

You can also use the Screen of Green method to limit your height (ScrOG). ScrOG is the use of a metal wire screen with squares ranging in size from 3" to 6" in size and mounting them horizontally above the plants at the desired height to help limit your plants' vertical growth.

85

At any time of day, you may set the electronic timer to the 12/12 blooming cycle. All you have to do is avoid entering the grow chamber during the dark time since any light will disturb the dark cycle, slowing down the blooming process.

Your marijuana plants will begin to exhibit sex 10 to 14 days after switching to the 12/12 lighting cycle. If you don't need seeds, wait until the sex is confirmed, then clip all-male plants at the root. Do not remove the male plants since their roots are all entangled and pulling them apart may cause harm.

If you want to have seeds, eliminate all-male plants and save the healthy, attractive ones. Breeding males and females of different strains may result from infertile seeds. The male blooms will begin to open and discharge pollen after a few days.

By permitting just 14 of the male flowers to open, pollens are dispersed. You may now take the male flowers out of the grow chamber. This will leave some female flowers unpollinated, resulting in an excellent balance of THC and seed production.

How To Tell If Your Marijuana Is Ready for Harvest

89

Use the following ways to determine if your weed is ready for harvest:

The Stigma Approach

Harvest your cannabis when the stigmas of your plants become orange but before they begin to turn brown. This enables the greatest possible concentration of THC and other chemical components. Because stigmas are visible to the naked eye, this approach eliminates the need for a magnifying lens.

The Trichomes Technique

To view the Trichomes clearly, you'll need a magnifying glass. The Trichomes will seem clear at first, then hazy, and lastly amber. While harvested when the Trichomes are hazy, the marijuana

91

produces an intense head high. While you pick your plants when the Trichomes are clouded, the marijuana will offer you a physical high. Mix 50/50 hazy and amber Trichomes to create a cannabis blend that provides a head and body high.

Your marijuana will be ready for harvest at this time, and you will be able to enjoy the fruits of your effort. You will get a lot of high-quality medical-grade

cannabis.

93

Conclusion

Thank you for downloading this book once again!

There is no question that if you follow the numerous ideas and tactics we have mentioned in this tutorial, you will have top-grade, indoor-produced, dank marijuana.

95